WORKBOOK
HARMONY AND VOICE LEADING
VOLUME 2
SECOND EDITION

WORKBOOK

HARMONY

AND
VOICE
LEADING

VOLUME 2

SECOND EDITION

EDWARD ALDWELL
The Curtis Institute of Music
The Mannes College of Music

CARL SCHACHTER
Queens College of the City University of New York

Harcourt Brace Jovanovich College Publishers
Fort Worth   Philadelphia   San Diego   New York   Orlando   Austin   San Antonio
Toronto   Montreal   London   Sydney   Tokyo

ISBN: 0-15-531521-8
Library of Congress Card Number: 88-80627
Printed in the United States of America

0 1 2 3 4 5 066 16 15 14 13 12

PREFACE

This workbook, together with the exercises in the text, should provide more than enough material for homework assignments, classroom demonstrations, and periodic reviews. It also provides a generous assortment of excerpts from the literature for assignments in analysis. Naturally, the number and type of exercises vary somewhat from unit to unit, depending on the material covered. Thus the exercises for the opening units are intended mainly as a review of the fundamental materials of tonal music. Their purpose is to give the student, as rapidly as possible, a secure grasp of scales, key signatures, intervals, and chords. Although *Harmony and Voice Leading* is not intended as an introduction to fundamentals, there is probably enough material in the workbook for a one-semester course in basic musicianship, if the instructor wishes to use it for that purpose.

Starting with Unit 6, the exercises in both the text and the workbook begin with a series of short drills, called Preliminaries. These form a concentrated review of the most important topics discussed in the unit. The drills are not always easy, but doing them well will give the student the necessary technical foundation for the longer and musically more interesting exercises that follow. If a class falls behind schedule, the instructor could save time by occasionally assigning only the preliminary drills before going on to the next unit. But a steady regimen of these exercises alone is not recommended.

The longer exercises are of various types, but most of them are melodies and basses (both figured and unfigured). It is now almost eighty years since Arnold Schoenberg decried the use of such exercises, but most harmony textbooks continue to include them, and most instructors continue to assign them. And with very good reason. There is no better way for the student to become aware of the interdependence of the elements of music—how a bass and a soprano combine to form good counterpoint, and how this counterpoint relates to harmonic progression.

A typical homework assignment might well consist of a melody and a bass; for this reason we have interspersed the two rather than separating them. For most units there are two groups of melodies and basses; those in the second group tend to be more difficult than those in the first. We might mention that, once past the beginning stages, students can benefit greatly from working out—and writing out—many solutions to an exercise, trying to determine the good and bad points of each, and deciding which is the best.

The excerpts from the literature, which begin with Unit 7, are suitable for analysis at sight during the classroom hour as well as for homework. As much as possible, students should do more than merely label the chords; they should concentrate on how the chords function, and they should be able to specify the techniques discussed in the unit that are exemplified in each of these excerpts.

E. A.

C. S.

CONTENTS

LIST OF STUDY AND ANALYSIS EXAMPLES

		Unit	No.
Haydn	Fantasia, Hob. XVII/4	31	1
Haydn	String Quartet, Op. 20/5, IV	23	1
Haydn	String Quartet, Op. 74/3, II	29	4
Haydn	String Quartet, Op. 77/2, IV	30	1
Liszt	A Faust Symphony (1853/4), I	31	8
Liszt	Consolation No. 3	32	7
Liszt	Ich scheide (1860)	30	9
Liszt	Liebestraum No. 3	27	5
Liszt	Sonetto 104 del Petrarca	30	8
Liszt	Tarantella, from Venezia e Napoli (1861)	30	10
Mendelssohn	A Midsummer Night's Dream, Op. 61, Wedding March	26	4
Mendelssohn	Song without Words, Op. 62/1	26	5
Mendelssohn	Song without Words, Op. 102/2	27	3
Mendelssohn	Variations, Op. 82, Variation I	23	4
Mozart	Clarinet Trio, K. 498, I	32	1
Mozart	Clarinet Trio, K. 498, I	20	3
Mozart	Menuett, K. 355	30	2
Mozart	Piano Concerto, K. 271, I, cadenza	29	1
Mozart	Piano Concerto, K. 271, II	31	2
Mozart	Piano Concerto, K. 503, I	22	1
Mozart	Piano Sonata, K. 533, I	29	2
Mozart	Piano Sonata, K. 533, I	31	4
Mozart	Piano Sonata, K. 576, II	29	3
Mozart	Sinfonia Concertante, K. 364, III	31	3
Mozart	String Quartet, K. 593, I	25	3
Mozart	The Magic Flute, K. 620, Act II	24	5
Mozart	Variations on an original theme, K. 54	25	2
Mozart	Violin Sonata, K. 296, III	26	3
Mozart	Violin Sonata, K. 526, III	28	2
Rossini	Petite Messe Solennelle, Credo	29	7
Schubert	Schwanengesang, D. 957, Der Doppelgänger	29	8
Schubert	Die Forelle, D. 550	25	5
Schubert	Die Liebe hat gelogen, D. 751	30	4
Schubert	Die Rose, D. 745	23	3
Schubert	Die schöne Müllerin, D. 795, Die liebe Farbe	22	2
Schubert	Winterreise, D. 911, Gute Nacht	24	6
Schubert	Octet, D. 803, I	30	3
Schubert	Octet, D. 803, VI	31	5
Schubert	String Quintet, D. 956, I	32	5
Schubert	"Wanderer" Fantasy, D. 760, I	20	5
Schumann	Carnaval, Op. 9, Eusebius	20	6
Schumann	Carnaval, Op. 9, Reconnaissance	31	6
Schumann	Humoreske, Op. 20, I	32	6
Schumann	Kinderscenen, Op. 15, Hasche-Mann	20	7
Schumann	Nachtstück, Op. 23/2	25	6
Schumann	Novellette, Op. 21/8	24	7
Schumann	Piano Concerto, Op. 54, I, cadenza	29	9
Schumann	Symphony No. 2, Op. 61, IV	27	4
Smetana	String Quartet ("Aus meinem Leben"), II	27	7
Verdi	Don Carlo, Aria, O Don Fatale	30	13
Verdi	La Forza del Destino, Overture	25	7

20
Melodic Figuration

PRELIMINARIES

Adding Tones of Figuration

1. Add figuration to the lower three voices of the Bach chorale below, including chordal skips and accented and unaccented passing tones and neighbors. (Keep in mind that using accented figuration will alter the position of some of the printed notes.) Don't worry about the unfamiliar chords; the purpose of this exercise is practice in adding tones of figuration.

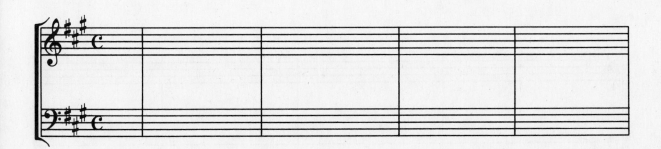

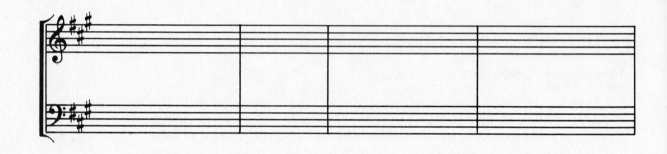

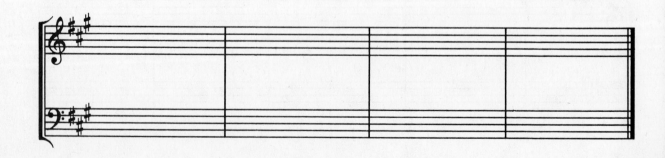

2. OUTER VOICES. Set for four voices, adding figuration (including incomplete neighbors, chromatic passing tones and neighbors, accented passing tones and neighbors, chordal skips, and so forth) to the *soprano.* Maintain throughout the eighth-note rhythm begun in bar 1.

4 LONGER ASSIGNMENTS

Melodies and Basses

1. FIGURED BASS. This exercise uses accented passing tones in the bass. Be sure you understand what each figure means; remember that the figure $^6_4$ doesn't always stand for an inversion of a seventh chord.

2. OUTER VOICES. Add the inner voices and label all tones of figuration in all voices.

NAME _____

6

3. MELODY. Set in four voices for piano or strings. The setting need not be restricted to vocal ranges and its bass rhythm may vary (sometimes just a dotted half). Label all tones of figuration (remember that some of them will be accented). Do *not* add figuration to the lower three voices.

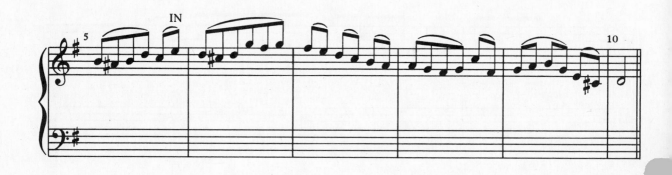

STUDY AND ANALYSIS

1. Excerpts from Bach chorales

Label and be able to explain all tones of figuration. Don't worry about unfamiliar chords.

(a) No. 96

*not I$^6_4$; why?   *7th transfers to and resolves in bass.

(b) No. 99

(c) No. 111

(d) No. 122

2. Excerpts from Bach chorale preludes

(a) Herr Gott, nun schleuss den Himmel auf, BWV 617

*Where does this D♯ resolve?

(b) Ach wie nichtig, ach wie flüchtig, BWV 644

3. Mozart, Clarinet Trio, K. 498, I

Explain the "parallel 5ths."

4. Beethoven, Violin Sonata, Op. 24, I

Discuss the use of the turn figure.

5. Schubert, "Wanderer" Fantasy, D. 760, I

(Allegro con fuoco ma non troppo)

6. Schumann, Eusebius, from Carnaval, Op. 9

(The $^6_4$ chords in this example were explained in Unit 19.)

7. Schumann, Hasche-Mann, from Kinderscenen, Op. 15

8. Brahms, Intermezzo, Op. 116/2

Explain the "parallel 5ths."

21
Rhythmic Figuration

PRELIMINARIES

Adding Suspensions

Add suspensions and other figuration to the lower three voices of these excerpts from Bach chorales. Don't worry about the unfamiliar chords.

1.

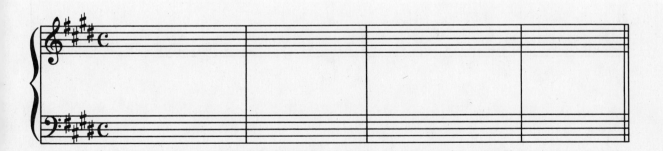

2.

3.

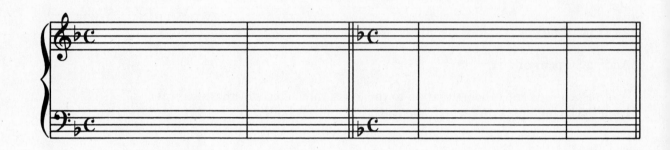

4.

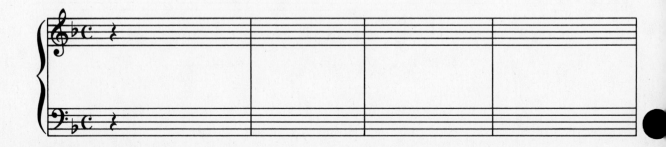

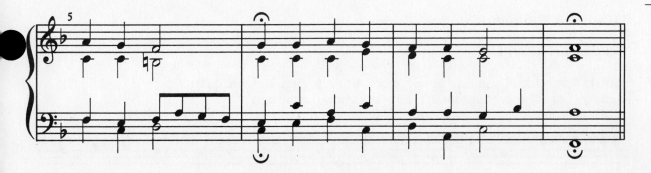

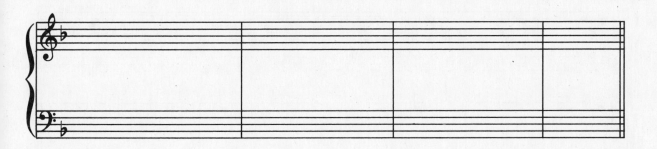

NAME _____

16 LONGER ASSIGNMENTS

Melodies and Basses 1

1. OUTER VOICES. Fill in the inner voices, using suspensions (in quarter-note rhythm only) where appropriate. Supply figures for the bass.

2. FIGURED BASS

3. OUTER VOICES

Melodies and Basses 2

1. FIGURED BASS

2. MELODY. Because of the quarter-note suspensions in the melody, the bass rhythm will often be in half notes. Where does the tonicization of V begin?

3. FIGURED BASS

Melodies and Basses 3

The following two exercises are adapted from Corelli. Both of them feature suspensions. In addition they contain other tones of figuration. A necessary first step in working them out is to determine which tones belong to the chords and which are passing or neighboring tones. For example, in the figured bass the first bar contains only two chords—the C♯ is a passing tone, the G♯ a neighbor. In the figured bass the numerous suspensions with their downward resolutions will tend to bring the upper voices into a low register. Look for appropriate opportunities to compensate for this tendency by leaping upward. These exercises should be done in keyboard style.

1. FIGURED BASS

NAME _____

20   **2. MELODY.** Set in keyboard style, using three voices where necessary. In bars 3½-4 the lower voices could imitate the soprano.

STUDY AND ANALYSIS

1. Excerpts from Bach chorales

Explain all tones of figuration.

(a) No. 121

*Explain the "parallel 5ths."

(last phrase)

(b) No. 128

*Explain the "parallel 5ths."

NAME _____

2. Bach, Well-Tempered Clavier II, Fugue 9

Beginning with bar 3½ indicate all suspensions and their resolutions. How many cadences are there? Are there avoided cadences? What makes them possible?

3. Bach, Cello Suite, BWV 1007, Trio of Menuet

This polyphonic melody suggests three voices. Are suspensions implied? Write out a realization in three voices on the staves provided.

4. Beethoven, Piano Sonata, Op. 27/2, III

Indicate all suspensions, direct and indirect.

5. Beethoven, Bagatelle, Op. 126/3

Analyze all chords and label tones of figuration. How do bars 28/29-35 and
35/36-43 relate to the rest of the piece? Look carefully for all pedal points.
How do they help to express the form?

*VII$^4_3$ V^6

* This chord is an applied diminished seventh to be discussed in Unit 25.

NAME _____

26   6. Brahms, Piano Concerto, Op. 15, II

Label all suspensions and anticipations. How does figuration play a role in forming the chords of the first half of bar 1? Are the rhythmic groupings and the notated meter always in agreement? Explain.

22
Mixture

PRELIMINARIES

Melodic Fragments and Unfigured Basses

Set for four voices. * indicates mixture.

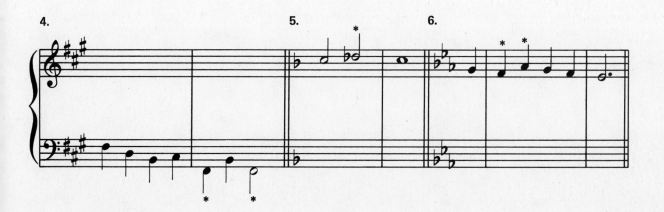

bass descends
in 3rds

LONGER ASSIGNMENTS

Melodies and Basses 1

1. OUTER VOICES. Set for string quartet.

2. MELODY

30   3. MELODY

Melodies and Basses 2

1. WALTZ. Use III#. The bass line of this exercise can repeat the same few tones almost throughout without creating a poor effect.

NAME _____

2. FIGURED BASS. Like the Corelli bass in Unit 21, this one contains figuration. Set in keyboard style; before you begin, review the instructions on page 19.

STUDY AND ANALYSIS

1. Mozart, Piano Concerto, K. 503, I

Provide figures for the bass. How is the phrase grouping affected by mixture?

(Allegro maestoso)

2. Schubert, Die liebe Farbe, from Die schöne Müllerin, D. 795

Where does the suspension in the beginning of bar 3 resolve?

In Grün will ich mich klei - den, in grü - ne Trä - nen -

wei - den: mein Schatz hat's Grün so gern, mein Schatz hat's Grün___ so gern.

translation: I will dress in green, in green weeping willows: my love likes green so much.

3. Brahms, Handel Variations, Op. 24, Variation 10

Reduce bars 1-4 to a simple progression in quarter notes without changes of register. Compare with the theme.

36   4. Verdi, La Traviata, Act III, No. 18

Compare the function of III♯ in bars 245-46 and 249-50. This excerpt contains interesting $^6_4$ usages. Indicate the function of all of them.

*Analyze the A♯ and C♯ as figuration.

translation: Ah, dear God! to die so young, I who have suffered so much!
To die so near to ending my unhappiness! Ah! hope, then, was a delusion!
My heart remained faithful in vain.

23
Leading-Tone Seventh Chords

PRELIMINARIES

Melodic Fragments

Use at least one leading-tone seventh chord in each of these fragments. Given bass tones may be repeated.

1. MINOR KEYS

38   2. MAJOR KEYS

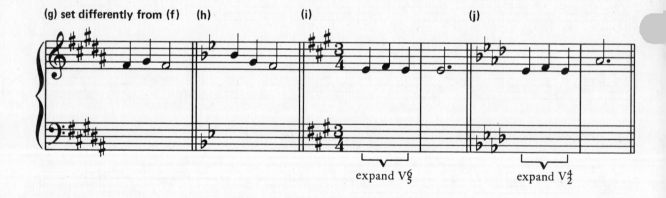

(g) set differently from (f)   (h)   (i)   (j)

expand V$^6_5$ expand V$^4_2$

LONGER ASSIGNMENTS

Melodies and Basses

1. MELODY

2. FIGURED BASS. The voice exchanges in bars 5-10 form a prominent feature of this exercise, hence the unusual figures in those bars.

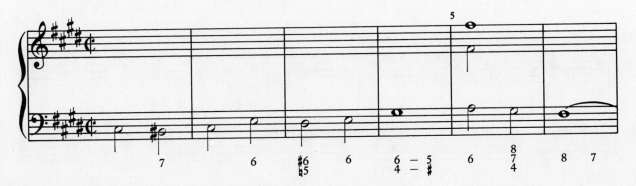

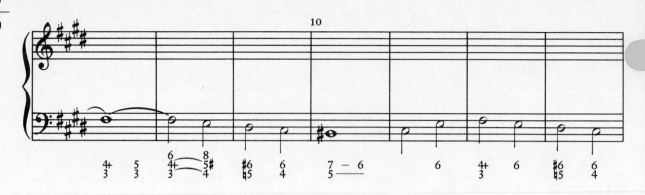

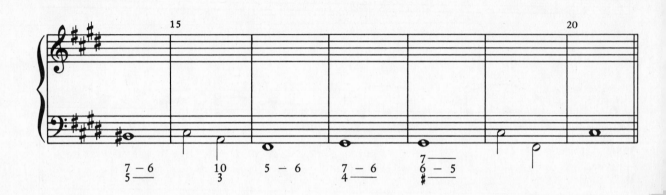

3. MELODY (adapted from Haydn). The middle section is in E♭ minor and ends with a Phrygian cadence. Both VII°⁷ and VII⌀⁷ are included.

Phrygian
cadence

susp.

NAME

STUDY AND ANALYSIS

1. Haydn, String Quartet, Op. 20/5, IV

How do bars 171-72 relate to 173-74? How do bars 177-80 relate to 171-74? How does the deceptive cadence prepare the harmonic change of the following phrase?

*This applied °7 chord will be discussed in Unit 25.

2. Beethoven, String Quartet, Op. 95, III

Analyze the first nine measures in C minor, and the remainder of the excerpt in F minor. The "C minor" of bars 1-9 tonicizes V of F minor. Relate bars 1-4 to bars 9-12. What is the function of the viola note on the first beat of bar 18?

3. Schubert, Die Rose

ich noch ster-bend sa - gen, wollt' ich noch ster-bend sa - gen.

translation: dying, I wanted to speak [of my brief, young life].

4. Mendelssohn, Variations, Op. 82, Variation 1

*VII° V

*To be discussed in Unit 25.

24
Remaining Uses of Seventh Chords

PRELIMINARIES

Seventh Chords in Sequence

Note that all of these progressions except (h) start with I.

(a)

(b) set differently from (a)

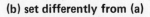

(c)

(d)

(e)

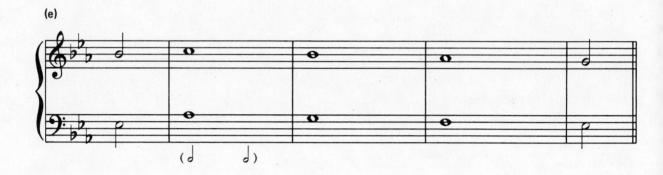

(f)

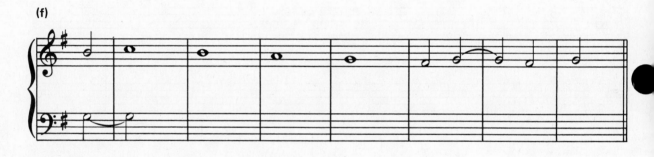

(g)

(h)

LONGER ASSIGNMENTS

Melodies and Basses 1

1. FIGURED BASS. Set for four voices. Extensive eighth-note figuration is possible (and desirable) in the soprano.

2. OUTER VOICES

3. MELODY. Every chord should be a seventh chord *except* in those places marked with an asterisk.

Melodies and Basses 2

1. OUTER VOICES. What seventh chord technique is used in this exercise?

52   **2. OUTER VOICES.** This exercise includes seventh chords extended through transferred 7ths, as well as transferred and delayed resolutions of 7ths.

3. MELODY * = apparent seventh chords.

bass and tenor:

dissonant
leap OK

* or *

inner voices:

NAME _____

24
53

54   STUDY AND ANALYSIS 1

The three excerpts in this section contain seventh chords in sequence. In addition to labeling each chord, try to determine how the sequence functions in a larger context.

1. Bach, Organ Fugue ("Wedge"), BWV 548

*An applied V^7; see Unit 25.

2. Bach, Little Prelude, BWV 938

3. Bach, Harpsichord Concerto, BWV 1052, I

56   STUDY AND ANALYSIS 2

All the excerpts in this section contain transferred or delayed resolutions, pro-
longed 7ths or apparent seventh chords. Besides giving a harmonic analysis of
each seventh chord (real or apparent), label the dissonance and show where
it resolves.

4. Bach, Cantata 167, recitative

translation: And ponder, Christians, what God has done for you.

5. Mozart, The Magic Flute, K. 620, Act II

Dann_____ wie - der ei - ne Pa - pa - ge - na, Pa - pa -

ge - no, Pa - pa - ge - no,

ge - na, Pa - pa - ge - na, Pa - pa - ge - na, Pa - pa - ge - na!

Pa - pa - ge - no, Pa - pa - ge - no, Pa - pa - ge - no!

translation: First a little Papageno, then a little Papagena, then another Papageno, then another Papagena . . .

NAME _____

58   **6. Schubert, Gute Nacht, from Winterreise, D. 911**

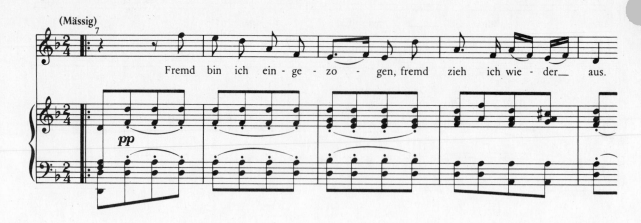

Fremd bin ich ein - ge - zo - gen, fremd zieh ich wie - der__ aus.

translation: A stranger I came here, a stranger I depart.

7. Schumann, Novellette, Op. 21/8

TRIO II
Hell und lustig

8. Chopin, Etude, Op. 10/12

*where does this F resolve?

25

Applied V and VII

PRELIMINARIES

Applied Chords 1

In four parts, write applied chords and their resolutions as indicated. *Important:* some of the chords of resolution will *not* be in root position; in these cases, add the appropriate figured-bass symbol to the roman numeral. (Note that the figures do *not* include accidentals.)

1. MAJOR KEYS

SAMPLE

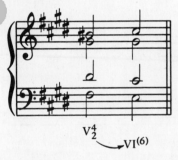

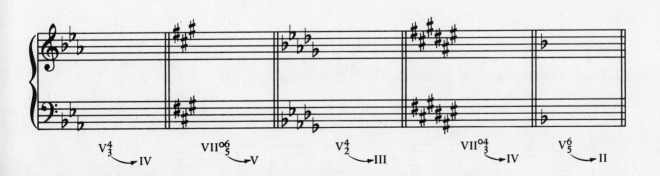

NAME _____

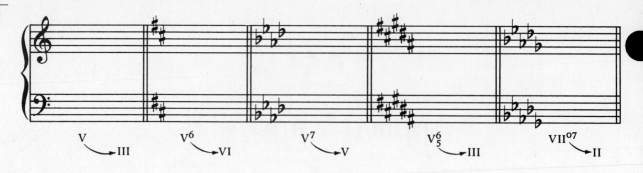

2. MINOR KEYS

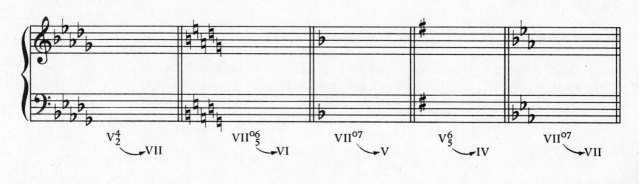

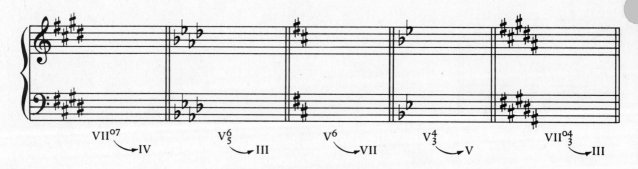

Applied Chords 2

1. Insert applied chords in places marked * to eliminate the parallel octaves.
   Continue to a cadence.

2. Insert an applied chord in the second half of bars 1-6 and fill in the inner voices.

3. Partially figured bass. Set for four parts in keyboard style, and supply the missing figures.

4. Insert applied V or VII chords in the indicated positions. The figures do *not* include accidentals!

64 LONGER ASSIGNMENTS

Melodies and Basses

1. UNFIGURED BASS. Set for four parts and supply figures.

2. CHORALE MELODY (Auf, Zion, auf!). * = applied chord.

3. FIGURED BASS. Add figuration if you like, especially in bars 6-8.

*Here the 7 (of 7-6) could be an incomplete neighbor.

4. MELODY. The bass will contain some chromatically altered tones. Use a "deceptive" applied chord at the asterisk in bar 8. Keyboard style is possible.

Melodies

1. Provide a simple four-part accompaniment, with applied chords at the asterisks.

Mozart (adapted)

2. Set for four string parts. The asterisks indicate applied chords, but not all of them are marked!

68 STUDY AND ANALYSIS

1. Excerpts from Bach chorales

(a) No. 105 (beginning)

(b) No. 108 (beginning)

(c) No. 108 (end)

2. Mozart, Variations on an original theme, K. 54 (1788)

VARIATION 3
(Allegretto)

(I)

3. Mozart, String Quintet, K. 593, I

(Allegro)

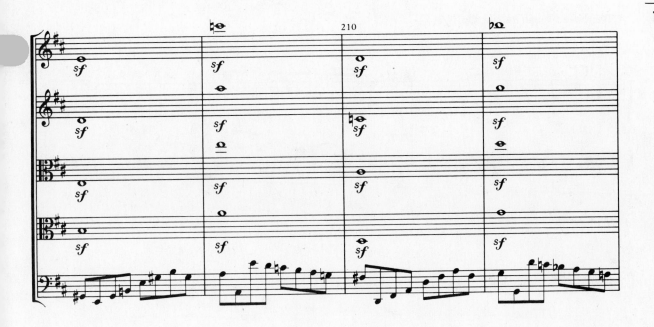

4. Beethoven, Piano Sonata, Op. 7, II

(Largo, con gran espressione)

5. Schubert, Die Forelle, D. 550

(Etwas lebhaft)

Doch end - lich ward dem Die - be

die Zeit zu lang. Er macht das Bäch - lein tük - kisch

cresc.

p   *cresc.*

*neighboring tone

trü - be, und eh⎯⎯ ich es ge-dacht, so zuck - te sei - ne

p

Ru - te, das Fisch - lein, das Fisch - lein zap - pelt dran, und

p

translation: But finally the thief grew impatient. Spitefully he muddied the stream, and before I knew it his fishing pole jumped and the fish struggled.

6. Schumann, Nachtstuck, Op. 23/2

7. Verdi, La Forza del Destino, Overture

140

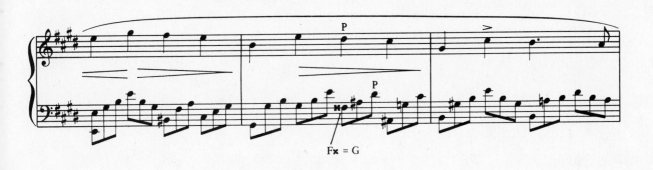

P

P

Fx = G

145

26
Diatonic Modulation

PRELIMINARIES

Modulating Melodic Fragments

Most of these fragments are taken from Bach chorales. As a first step, sketch in provisional cadences.

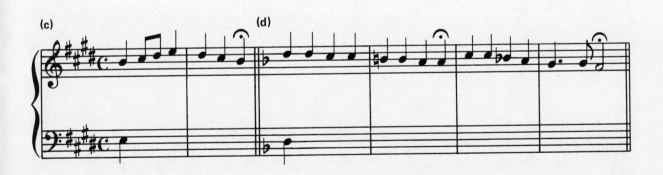

NAME _____

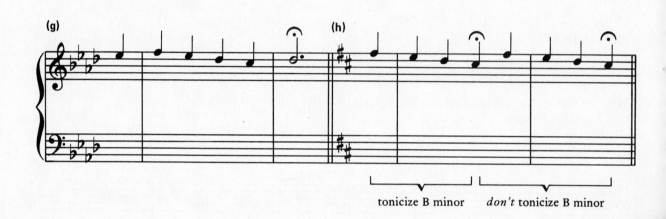

tonicize B minor   *don't* tonicize B minor

not the same cadence as in (k)

LONGER ASSIGNMENTS

Chorale Melodies

1. Don't harmonize the rests.

2. At the asterisk and at other cadences, harmonize the repeated notes with a repeated chord. In other places, the repeated notes might be harmonized by a single chord, possibly animated by eighth-note figuration in the bass.

NAME _____

3.

4.

NAME _____

82   Melodies and Basses

1. Complete bass and inner voices.

6 — 5   4 — 3   (♪♪♪)

2. Complete the keyboard setting.

Caldara (adapted)

NAME _____

84   3. Set for four voices.

4. **UNFIGURED BASS (mostly).** Set in four-part keyboard style. Two kinds of settings are possible for this bass: one where the soprano moves mostly in halves and quarters; the other where the soprano moves mostly in eighths, using parallel 10ths, parallel 6ths, and contrary motion.

Fenaroli (adapted)

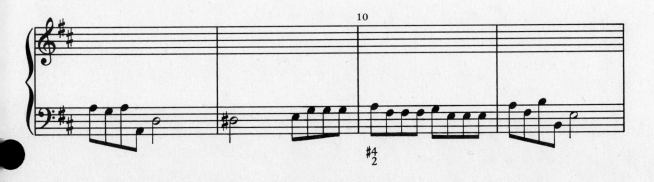

NAME _____

STUDY AND ANALYSIS

1. Bach chorales

(a) No. 263

(b) No. 269

(c) No. 274 (first half)

*Doesn't sound like $\frac{6}{4}$; in performance, instrumental bass is doubled at the lower octave.

2. Bach, Orchestral Suite No. 1, Menuet II

What is the function of the tonicizations following the double bar?

NAME _____

90   3. Mozart, Violin Sonata, K. 296, III

This movement is written in a kind of rondo form (ABACBA). The excerpt shows the second A section, the C section, and the beginning of the second B section.

94   **4. Mendelssohn, Wedding March (from A Midsummer Night's Dream, Op. 61)**

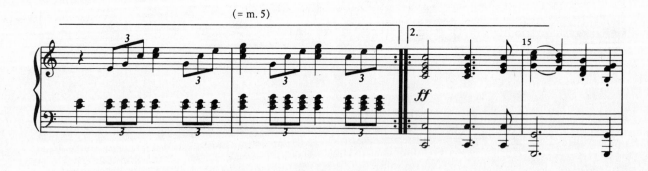

5. Mendelssohn, Song without Words, Op. 62/I

To what goal does the passage that begins in bar 10½ lead? Is there a key that contains as diatonic elements all the chords on the downbeats of this passage?

*Augmented 6th chord (Unit 29)

27

Seventh Chords with
Added Dissonance

PRELIMINARIES

Melodic Fragments

Set for four voices, using major except as indicated. * = dominant harmony.

98 LONGER ASSIGNMENTS

Melodies and Basses

1. OUTER VOICES. What is tonicized in bars 4-6?

2. WALTZ. Use free keyboard texture. Many, but not all, of the first-beat melody tones will form 9ths with the bass.

3. MELODY. Set in four-part instrumental style, using 9ths wherever practical.
Look for opportunities to use pedal points, both tonic and dominant.

Allegro molto

STUDY AND ANALYSIS

1. Bach, Well-Tempered Clavier II, Prelude 12

NAME _____

3. Mendelssohn, Song without Words, Op. 102/2

4. Schumann, Symphony No. 2, Op. 61, IV

(winds and brass omitted)

(Allegro, molto vivace)

5. Liszt, Liebestraum No. 3

(Poco allegro, con affetto)

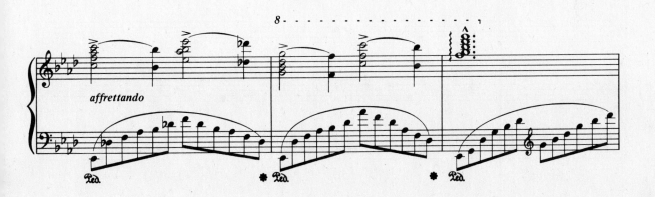

translation: [on] that day, that day of wrath, all shall crumble into ash.

Allegro moderato a la Polka

28

The Phrygian II (Neapolitan)

PRELIMINARIES

Melody and Bass-Line Fragments

Use ♭II⁶ (or ♭II⁵₃) wherever appropriate.

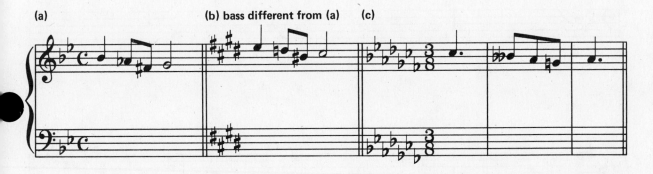

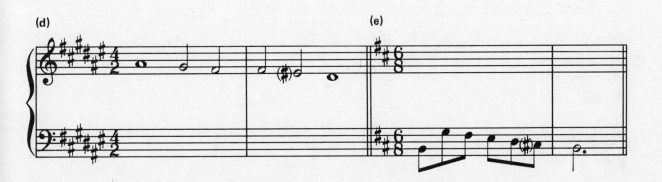

(f)

(g)　　　　　　　　　　　　　　　　　　(h)

(i)　　　　tonicize　　　　　　　　　(j)

(k) (modulates)　　　　　　　　　(l) (modulates)

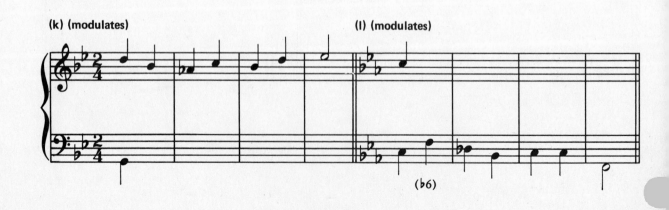

(♭6)

LONGER ASSIGNMENTS

Melodies and Basses

1. MELODY

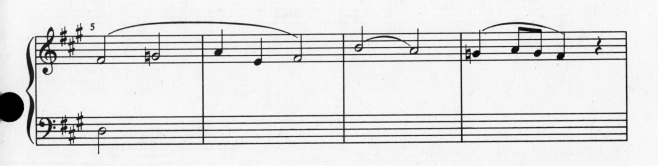

112 2. FIGURED BASS

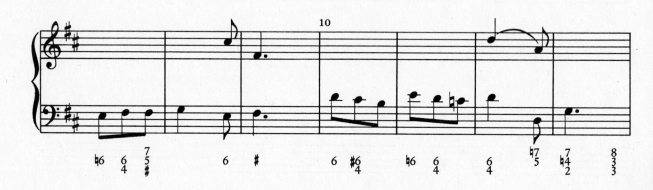

same upper voices
both measures

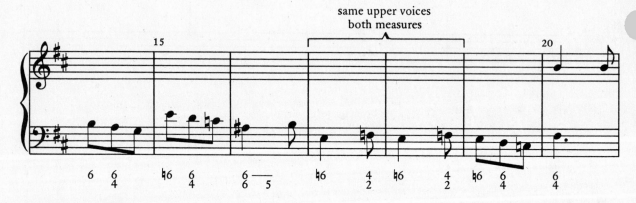

molto ritardando - - - - - - - - - - -

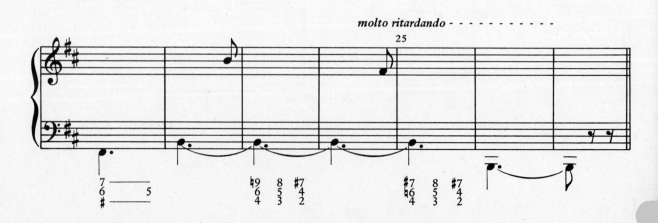

3. MELODY

NAME _____

STUDY AND ANALYSIS

1. Bach, St. Matthew Passion, Aria, Erbarme dich

(violin solo)

2. Mozart, Violin Sonata, K. 526, III

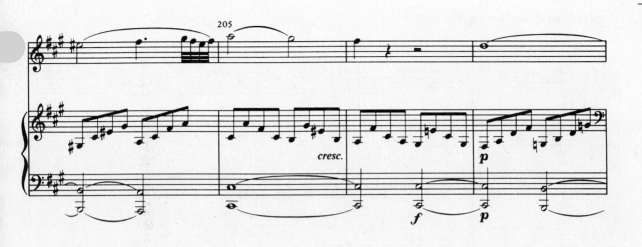

118   3. Beethoven, String Quartet, Op. 59/2, III

4. Chopin, Polonaise, Op. 40/2

5. Brahms, Capriccio, Op. 76/8

6. Brahms, Handel Variations, Op. 24, Variation 5

29

Augmented Sixth Chords

PRELIMINARIES

Melodic Fragments

Set in minor except as indicated. Use augmented sixth chords wherever appropriate.

(f)

(g) major

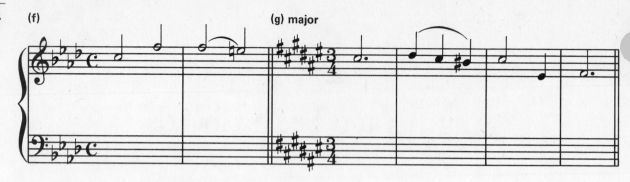

(h) major

(i)

ant.

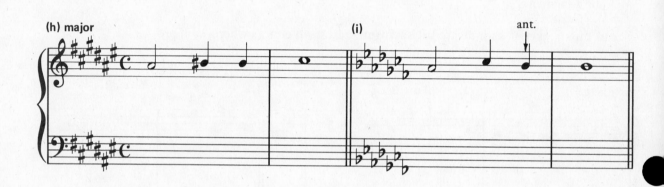

(j) major

(k) use diminished 3rd

LONGER ASSIGNMENTS

Melodies and Basses

1. MELODY. * = augmented 6th chord; ** = diminished 3rd chord.

126 2. FIGURED BASS

3. MELODY

128 STUDY AND ANALYSIS

1. Mozart, Piano Concerto, K. 271, I, cadenza

2. Mozart, Piano Sonata, K. 533, I

3. Mozart, Piano Sonata, K. 576, II

4. Haydn, String Quartet, Op. 74/3, II

(a)

(b)

5. Beethoven, Symphony No. 3, Op. 55, II (Marcia funebre)

6. Beethoven, Piano Sonata, Op. 57 ("Appassionata"), II

7. Rossini, Petite Messe Solennelle, Credo

132 8. Schubert, Der Doppelganger

Compare (a) with (b).

(a) (Sehr langsam)

in die - sem_ Hau - se wohn - te mein_ Schatz;

(b)

und ringt die Hän - de vor Schmer - zens - ge - walt;____

translation: (a) in this house lived my love.
(b) and wrings his hands in agony.

9. Schumann, Piano Concerto, Op. 54, I

The entire cadenza (too long to quote here) would be a valuable study.

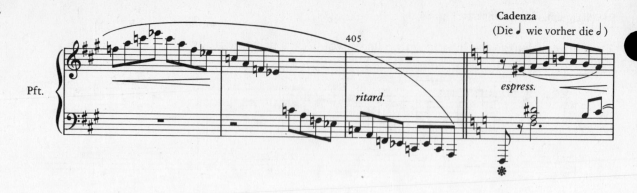

10. Chopin, Tarantelle, Op. 43

11. Brahms, Nachtigall, Op. 97/I

translation: In your song a quiet echo (of tones that died away long ago)!

30
Other Chromatic Chords

PRELIMINARIES

Mixture

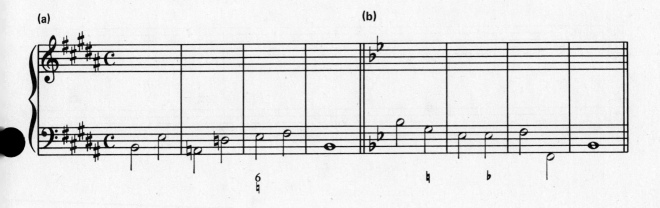

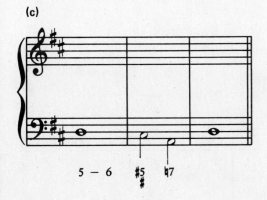

138 **COMMON-TONE DIMINISHED SEVENTH CHORDS.** Insert a °7 chord where indicated by asterisk. Not all are common-tone chords. Note the °7's in the way that most clearly indicates their function.

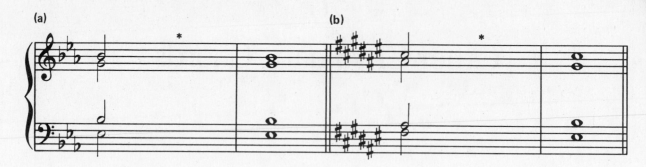

AUGMENTED TRIADS. Insert an augmented triad where indicated by asterisk. In some cases the augmented triad is produced by simple figuration; in other cases the chord changes entirely.

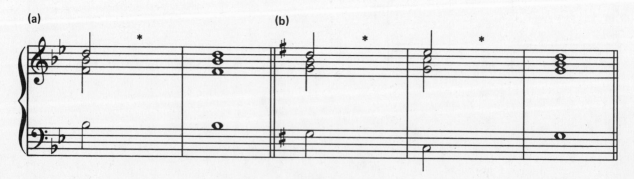

(c)

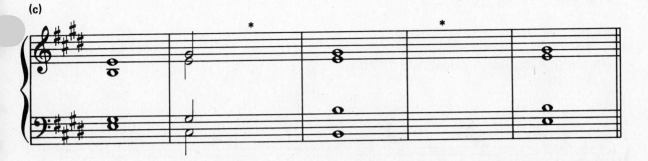

OTHER CHROMATIC CHORDS ($V_{5\sharp}^7$, $V_{5\flat}^7$, common-tone "dominant sevenths" and "augmented sixths"). Insert chords where indicated by asterisk. Use different progressions in a, b, and c.

(a)   **(b)**   **(c)**

(d)   **(e)**

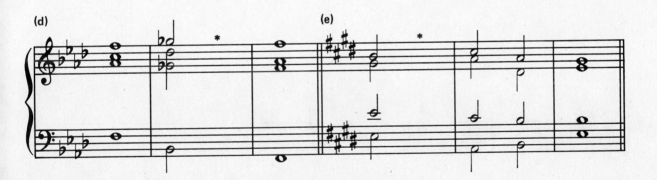

140　**LONGER ASSIGNMENTS**

Melodies and Basses

1. FIGURED BASS, USING AUGMENTED TRIADS

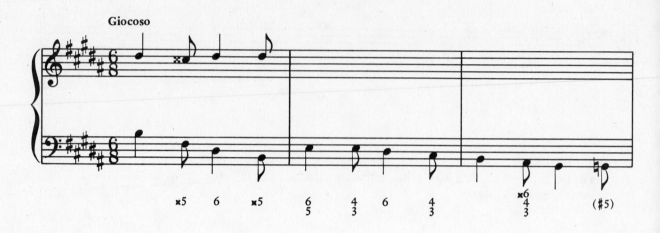

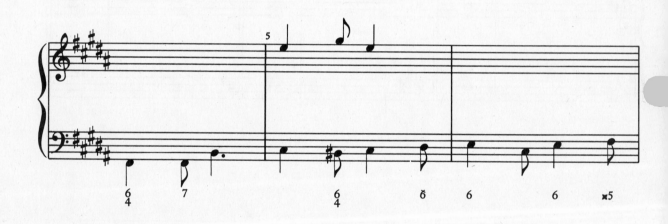

2. MELODY. Use common-tone °7th chords wherever appropriate. Keyboard style is possible.

Lugubre e pesante

4. MELODY. Set in free keyboard style.

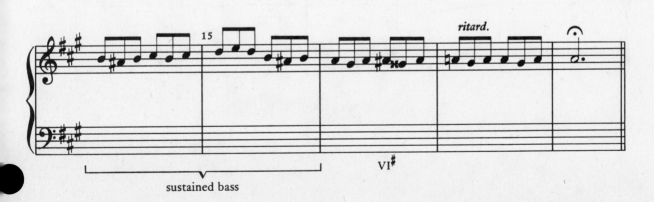

144 STUDY AND ANALYSIS

1. Haydn, String Quartet, Op. 77/2, IV

2. Mozart, Menuett, K. 355

3. Schubert, Octet, D. 803, I

146   4. Schubert, Die Liebe hat gelogen

Die Lie-be hat ge-lo-gen, die Sor-ge la-stet schwer, be-

tro - gen, ach! be-tro - gen hat al - les mich um - her!

translation: Love has lied, grief weighs heavy; ah, everything around me has betrayed me!

5. Chopin, Nocturne, Op. 27/1

6. Chopin, Prelude, Op. 28/5

(Allegro molto)

7. Chopin, Polonaise, Op. 44

8. Liszt, Sonetto 104 del Petrarca

(Adagio) *molto espressivo*

NAME _____

9. Liszt, Ich scheide (1860)

translation: Farewell, I depart.

10. Liszt, Tarantella, from Venezia e Napoli (1861)

11. Wagner, Tristan und Isolde, Act III, Scene 1

translation: Through the dawn, [the melody sounded] sad and sadder, as the
son learned his mother's fate.

12. Wagner, Tristan und Isolde, Act III, Scene 1

13. Verdi, Don Carlo, Aria, O Don Fatale

translation: Alone in a cloister, hidden from the world, I can hide my despair.

31
Chromatic Voice-Leading Techniques

PRELIMINARIES

Unfigured Basses

1. Progressions based on parallel motion.

(a)

(b) different from (a)

(c) different from (a) and (b)

NAME _____

(d)

(e)

(f) different from (e)

(g)

(h)

(i) different from (h)

2. Progressions based on contrary motion.

(a)

(b)

(c)

(d)

(e)

LONGER ASSIGNMENTS

Melodies

1. "QUASI RECITATIVO." Set for violin and piano. Explain the function of the
tonicized C♯ minor chord in bars 9-11.

NAME _____

2. MELODY. Set for keyboard, maintaining the two-part broken-chord texture
of the first phrase.

NAME _____

158 3. **MELODY (mostly).** Set for piano, continuing the pattern of the first measure. The left-hand inner voice need not be maintained throughout and the left hand may play octaves. Octave doublings may occur between the bass and one of the inner voices.

(voice exchange between bass and inner voice)

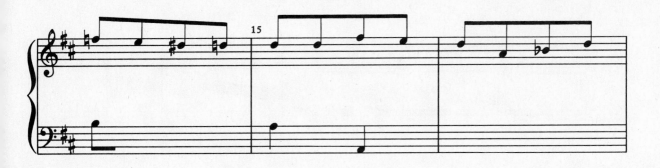

NAME _____

160   STUDY AND ANALYSIS

1. Haydn, Fantasia, Hob. XVII/4

2. Mozart, Piano Concerto, K. 271, II

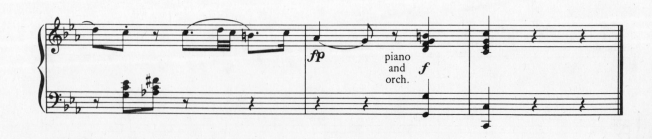

3. Mozart, Sinfonia Concertante, K. 364, III

162   4. Mozart, Piano Sonata, K. 533, I

5. Schubert, Octet, D. 803, VI

(Allegro)

164   6. Schumann, Reconnaissance, from Carnaval, Op. 9

7. Chopin, Nocturne, Op. 27/2

9. Wagner, Tristan und Isolde, Act II, Duet

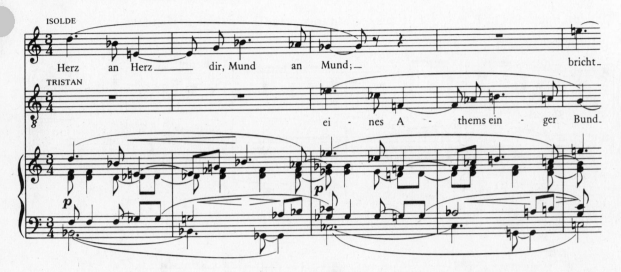

translation: Heart to heart, mouth to mouth, united in a single breath . . .

10. Wolf, Herr, was trägt der Boden

Although the song as a whole is in E minor, analyze these first six bars in B minor. What contrapuntal technique forms the basis of this passage?

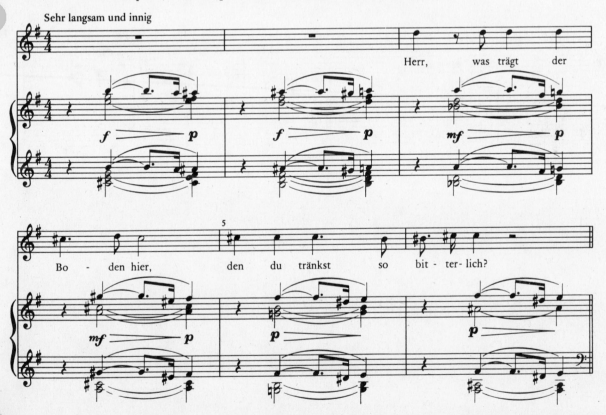

translation: Lord, what grows here that you water with such bitter tears?

168   11. Brahms, Intermezzo, Op. 119/I

This intermezzo is in B minor, but this section tonicizes III. Analyze as if in D.

32

Chromaticism in Larger Contexts

PRELIMINARIES

Modulating Fragments

Set for four voices.

* = °7 chord.

NAME _____

170

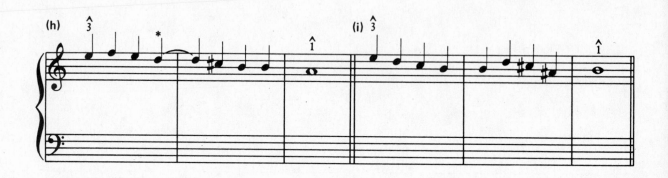

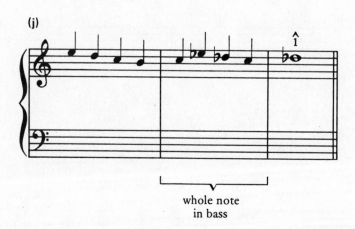

whole note
in bass

LONGER ASSIGNMENTS

Melodies and Basses

1. MELODY. Maintain the given accompaniment pattern of mostly one chord per measure throughout most of the piece. How do the modulations to E major and D major relate to the tonality of D♭?

NAME _____

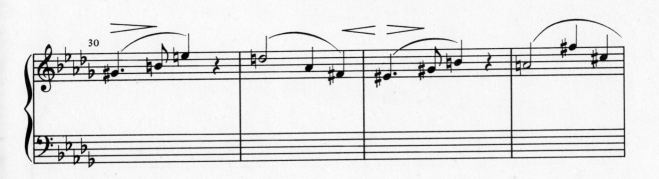

(tonic pedal)

174   **2. FIGURED BASS (by Padre Mattei).** Set for four voices. What is the large-scale tonal plan of this bass?

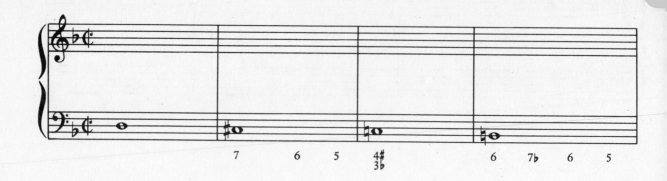

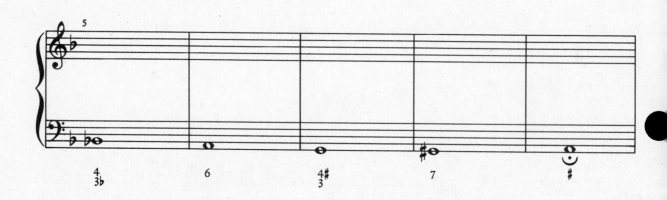

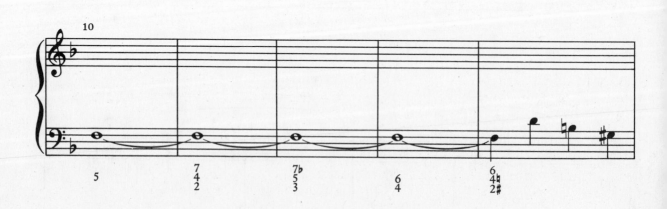

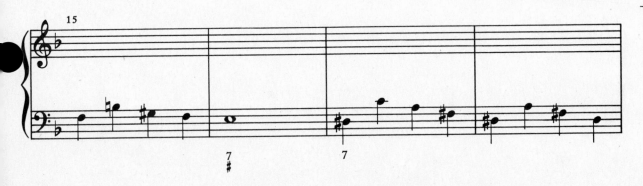

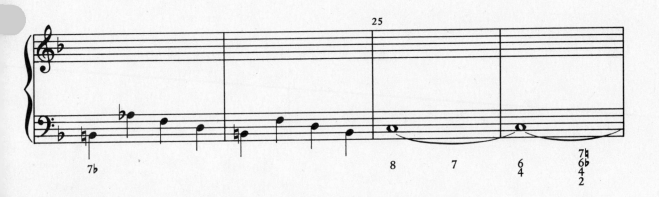

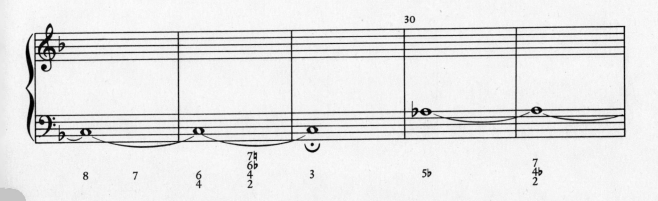

NAME _____

32

176

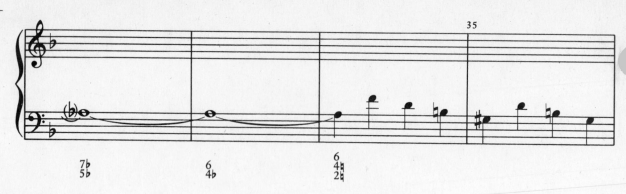

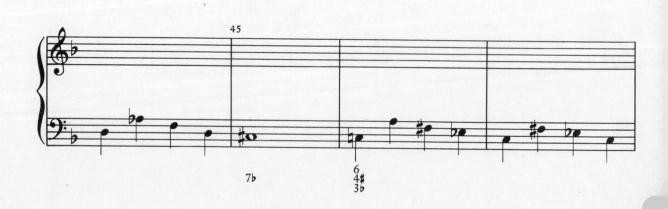

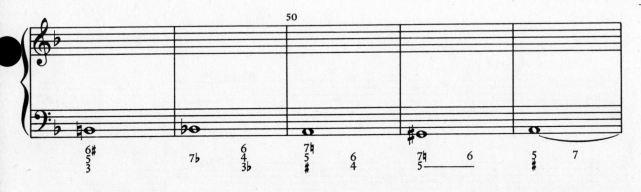

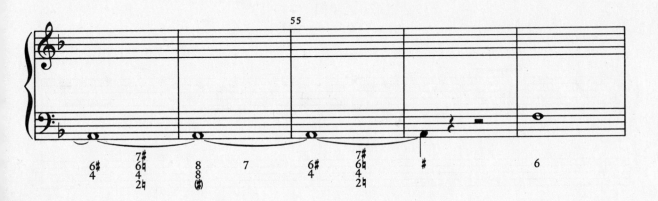

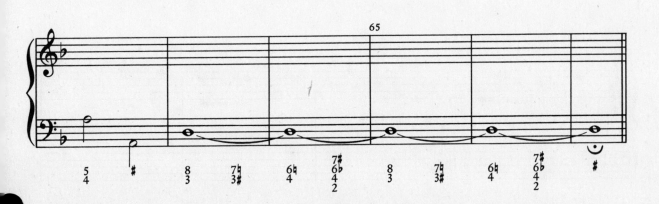

178   **3. MELODY.** Set in keyboard style; the right hand plays only the melodic line.

STUDY AND ANALYSIS

1. Mozart, Clarinet Trio, K. 498, I

(end of development)

182 2. Beethoven, Piano Sonata, Op. 26, III

MARCIA FUNEBRE sulla morte d'un Eroe

Maestoso andante

3. Beethoven, Piano Sonata, Op. 110, I

184   4. Beethoven, Piano Sonata, Op. 110, III

5. Schubert, String Quintet, D. 956, I

(Allegro ma non troppo)

NAME _____

186 6. Schumann, Humoreske, Op. 20, I

7. Liszt, Consolation No. 3

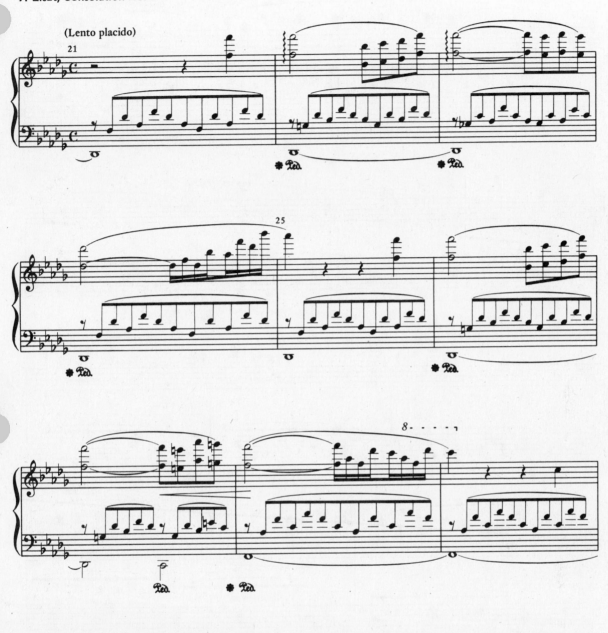